MY FIRST OUTDOOR GARDEN

Everything You Need to Know to Plant and Grow Your Own Fruits, Vegetables, and Flowers

To my son, Thanchan,
whom I love two billions...

Sky Pony Press books may be purchased in bulk at special discounts for sales promotion, corporate gifts, fund-raising, or educational purposes. Special editions can also be created to specifications. For details, contact the Special Sales Department, Sky Pony Press, 307 West 36th Street, 11th Floor, New York, NY 10018 or info@skyhorsepublishing.com.

Sky Pony® is a registered trademark of Skyhorse Publishing, Inc.®, a Delaware corporation.
Visit our website at www.skyponypress.com.

10 9 8 7 6 5 4 3 2 1

Manufactured in China, September 2021
This product conforms to CPSIA 2008

Library of Congress Cataloging-in-Publication Data is available on file.

Cover design provided by Éditions Rustica
Cover illustration by Charlène Tong

Print ISBN: 978-1-5107-6395-1
Ebook ISBN: 978-1-5107-6396-8

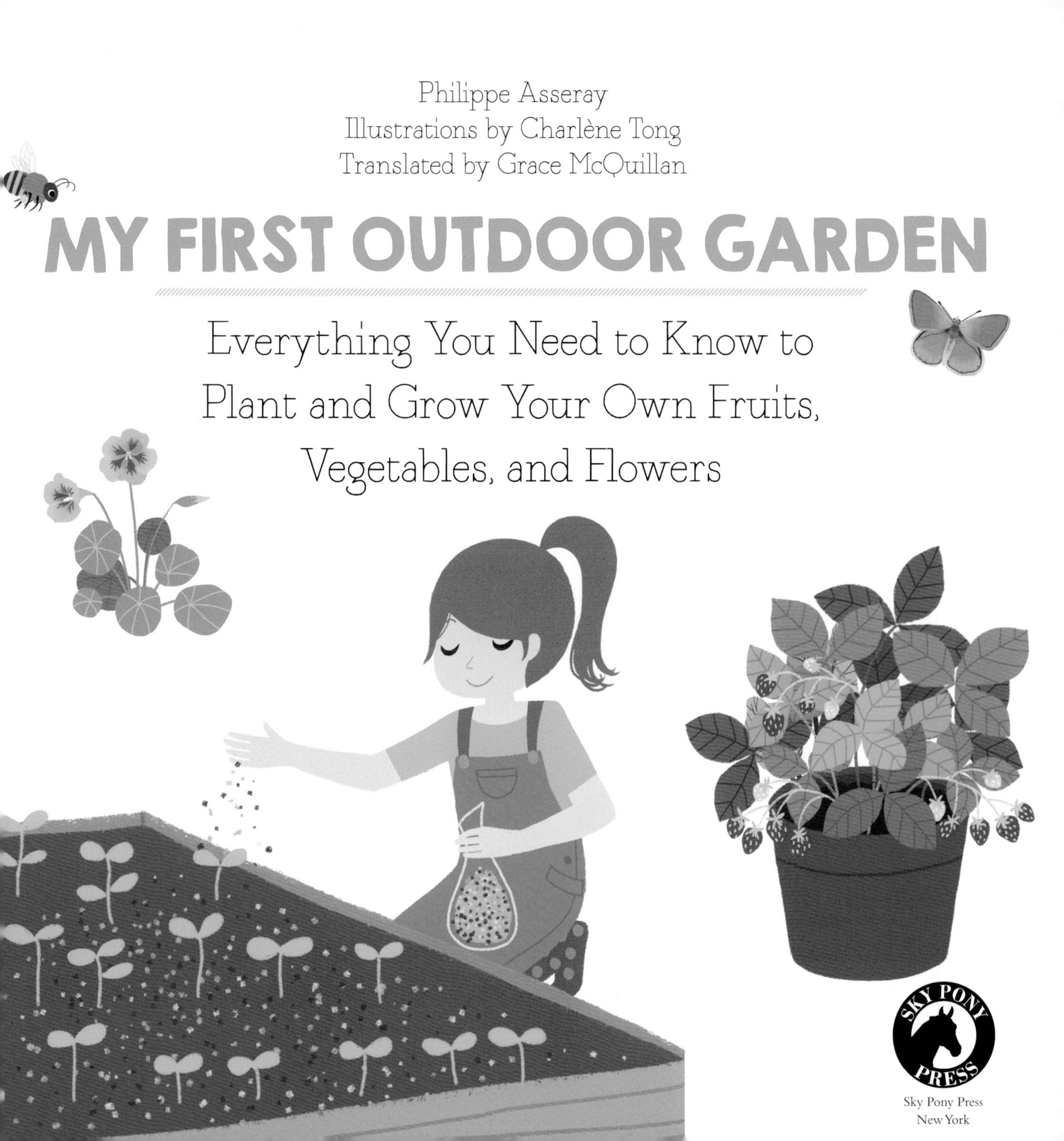

Philippe Asseray
Illustrations by Charlène Tong
Translated by Grace McQuillan

MY FIRST OUTDOOR GARDEN

Everything You Need to Know to Plant and Grow Your Own Fruits, Vegetables, and Flowers

Sky Pony Press
New York

CONTENTS

Tools I Need 6
Colorful handles 9

Building My Box Garden 10
Support for climbing plants 12
My name on my box garden 13

What Kind of Soil Should I Use? 14
What makes a good gardening soil? 14
How can I make good gardening soil? 15
"Modeling clay" soil 16

Sowing Seeds 18
Planting carrot seeds 18
Planting green bean seeds 20
Seed ribbons and mats 22

Planting Flowers and Vegetables with Root Balls 24
Planting Swiss chard 24
Roots in a glass 27

Gardening with the Moon 28

Taking Cuttings 30
Taking geranium cuttings 30
A funny kind of cutting 32

Watering Without Wasting 34
Tips for watering my raised bed 34

Feeding My Plants 38
What kind of food should I give my plants? 38
Mussels and oysters on the menu 40

Making My Compost 42

Who Are These Visitors? 44
Building a scarecrow 46

Discovering Permaculture 48

Trivia 50

My Vegetables and Fruits 52

My Flowers 56

My Gardening Calendar 60

Index 62

TOOLS I NEED

Many stores sell gardening tools made for children. They're the right size for you and are much lighter than adult tools, but they are also much less sturdy. You will be better off using your parents' tools. With their permission, of course.

Pitch Fork

This tool has four tines, or teeth, that are thin and curved. Use it like a rake: push the tines into the ground and then pull the fork toward you. This helps break up clumps of roots in the soil. If your parents give you one, ask them to shorten the handle and tines to make it more your size.

Rake

This tool is used to smooth out the surface of the soil. Just like with the pitch fork, your parents could shorten the handle of an adult model to make it easier for you to use.

It's a little like a metal comb with a long handle.

Hoe

This is a tool with a different kind of metal blade on each side. One side is flat and rectangular, and the other is pointed and shaped like a tree leaf. With the rectangular end, you can pull up weeds and their roots. With the pointed side, you can trace a little furrow to plant your seeds.

Trowel

You can use this tool to dig holes for planting flower bulbs or any kind of plant that is sold in a small plastic pot called a "seed starter."

It looks like a little shovel.

Why do the roots need to be bare?

Because leeks and lettuce always grow better after a little "transplanting." Here's how it works: the vegetables are planted in one section of the garden and are carefully picked when they are 4 to 6 inches tall. Then they are replanted in rows right away—just as they are, bare roots and all—and you can watch them continue to grow!

Dibble

This is a pointy tool that you can stick straight into the ground to make narrow, deep holes. In these holes, you can plant leeks or lettuce plants that are sold with bare roots.

Watering Can

Ask your grown-ups to find you a small one; it will be easier for you to pick it up.

COLORFUL HANDLES

Ask your grown-ups for water-resistant wood paint in several different colors, a paintbrush, and a long apron to protect your clothes. You can paint the handles all one color or in different patterns, like the colorful sticks in a game of pick-up sticks.

1. Arrange your tools vertically by pushing them into the ground or by placing a stone on top of the metal end to hold each one in place.

2. Make sure there is no dirt on the wood. If you need to, ask your grown-ups if you can borrow an old sponge and clean the handles. Let dry completely.

3. Now paint the handles with an even layer of paint. There is no need to paint the metal ends.

BUILDING MY BOX GARDEN

You can help Mom and Dad anywhere in the yard when they're around—that goes without saying! But if you're gardening by yourself, it's better to have your own box garden (or raised bed) just for you. Here's what to do. Ask for help from an adult because some of the steps are a bit tricky.

- 4 wooden boards: 3¼ feet long, 6 inches wide, ¾ inch thick
- 8 metal brackets
- Wood screws
- A battery-powered electric screwdriver

1 Place the boards on their sides, end to end, to form a square. Make sure all of the boards are level.

This is heavy!

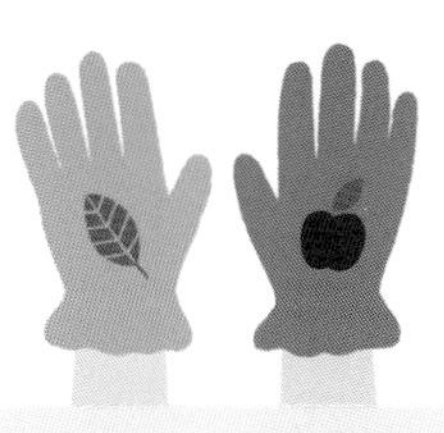

2 Place two brackets in each corner.

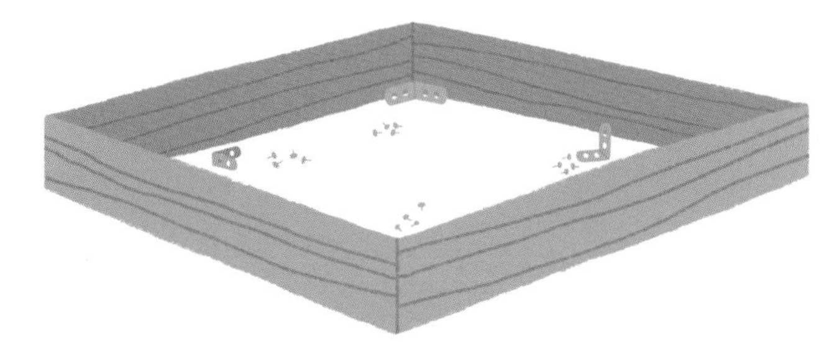

Watch out for splinters!

Wear gloves when handling the boards. They are made of rough wood, and you could get a splinter. This isn't very serious, but it is painful.

3 Attach the brackets with the screws using the electric screwdriver. You can ask for help if it is too hard. When your raised bed (or box garden) is assembled, ask an adult to carry it to its final destination.

Plants aren't afraid of getting sunburned.

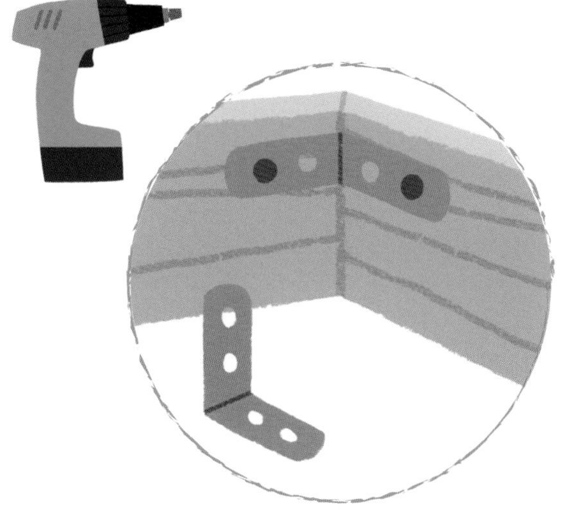

Where should I place my box garden?

Plants often need a lot of light, so avoid placing your outdoor garden under a tree. The best place is in the vegetable garden. There will be plenty of light and the soil in that area shouldn't be very hard, either.

SUPPORT FOR CLIMBING PLANTS

Build a trellis out of bamboo to place on one side of your outdoor garden. It can accommodate climbing flowers or even vegetables like beans. Ask for help to make sure everything holds together.

1. On the outside of the raised bed, choose a board and place one 4-foot bamboo stake at each corner. You may need a hammer to push them into the ground.

2. Hammer in the rest of the 4-foot bamboo stakes between these two corners. Leave about 8 inches between each stake.

3. Connect the tops with one horizontal bamboo stake 3½ feet long. Attach it using string, tying a square knot on each stake as shown below.

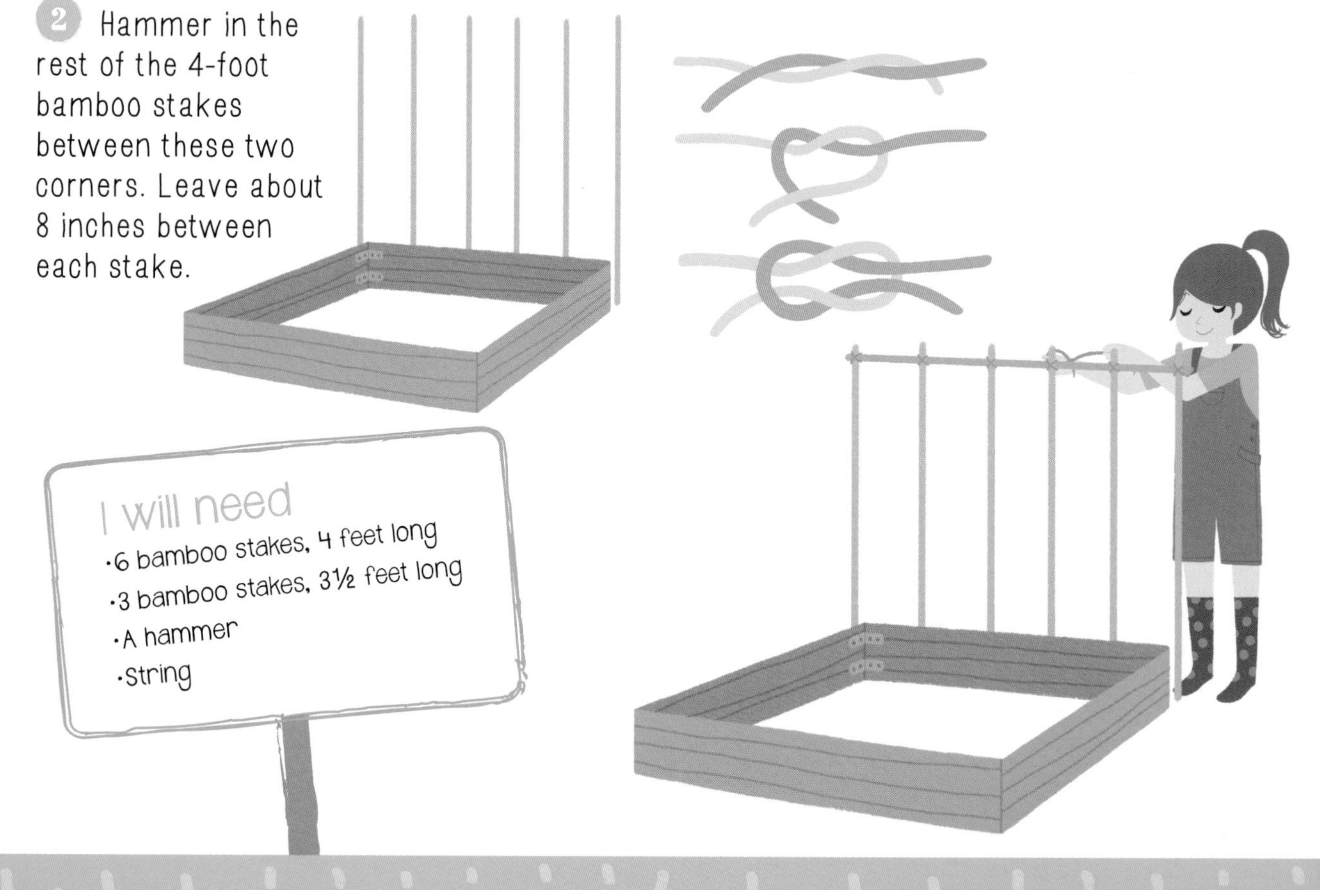

4 Attach another bamboo stake horizontally 8 inches below the first, then a third stake 8 inches below the second one.

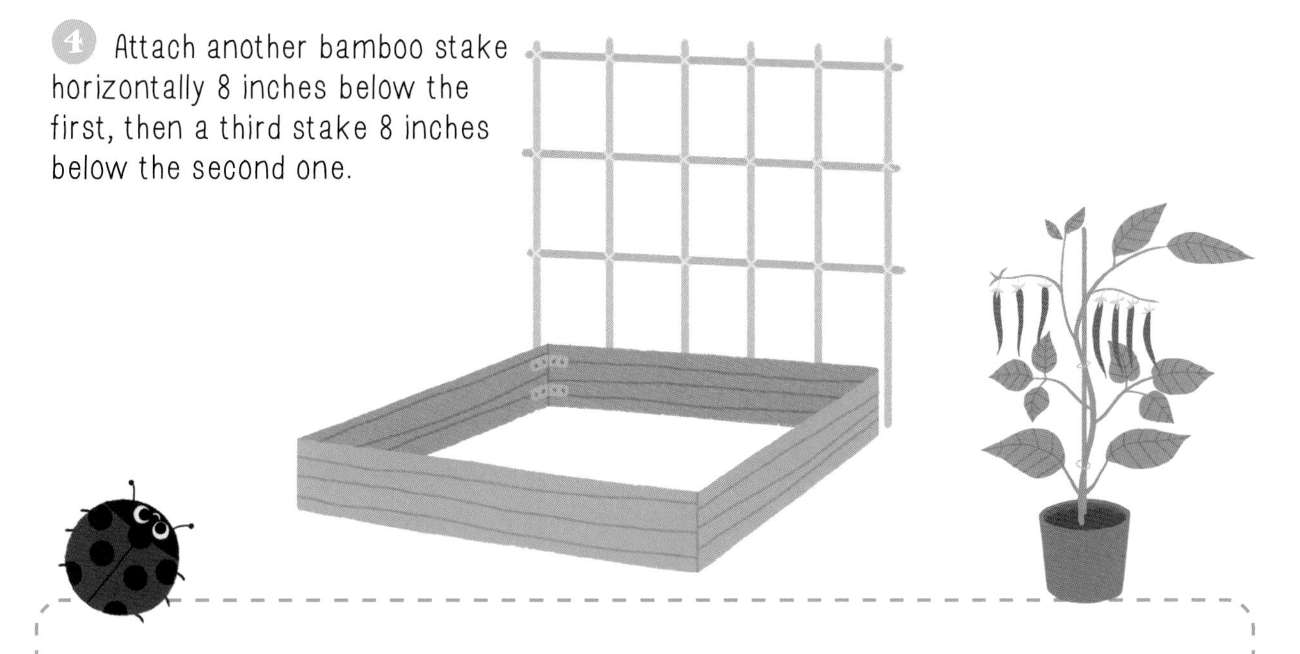

MY NAME ON MY BOX GARDEN

Make sure your box (or raised bed) garden is clearly marked to keep your dog or cat from coming to play in it!

Write your name on one of the boards using precut strips of wood to form the letters. You can then paint the letters any color you like. Attach the letters by nailing them together. You can also paint your name directly on the boards.

WHAT KIND OF SOIL SHOULD I USE?

The dirt in your grown-up's yard may be hard to work with using your small tools. Ask them to help you make a mixture similar to sand that you can use.

WHAT MAKES A GOOD GARDENING SOIL?

Good soil is not too hard, which means that gardeners can easily dig around in it and that the roots can spread out all by themselves to look for water and food.

Good soil also has small clods and even a few stones!

Small clods?
These are little balls of dirt made up of clay, sand, and humus. Water and air pass between the clods to reach the roots.

Most importantly, it should have earthworms. If the soil is good for them, it means it's good for gardening!

HOW CAN I MAKE GOOD GARDENING SOIL?

You will need an adult to go pick up bags of compost and carry them to your box garden. Ask an adult to loosen the dirt at the bottom of your raised bed with a pitch fork or rake.

1 Tear off the tops of the compost bags and dump the contents into your bed on top of the loosened dirt.

2 Use your pitch fork to mix the loosened dirt and compost.

I will need
- 3 (10.5-gallon) bags of compost
- A shovel
- A pitch fork

Don't fill your box garden all the way to the top. Leaving a little room will prevent the soil from overflowing when it rains or when you water.

"MODELING CLAY" SOIL

Test the dirt in your yard to find out what you can plant in it.

1 Take a handful of damp soil from your raised bed and knead it into a ball the size of an egg.

2 Next, roll this ball between your hands to make a sausage shape.

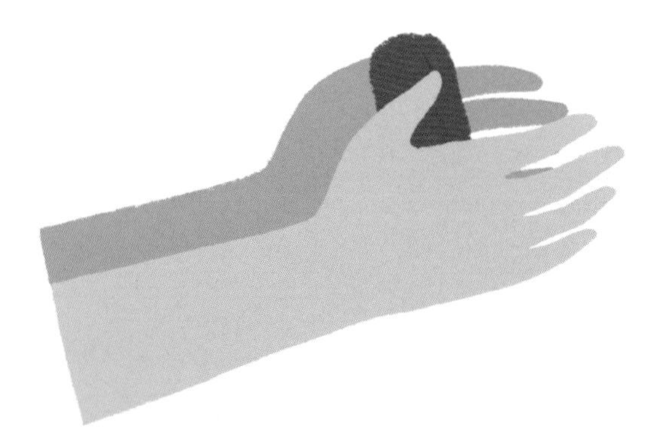

3 If you can't make the sausage shape because the soil keeps breaking apart, this means that the dirt does not have a lot of clay in it. It will be easy to work with, but you won't be able to grow radishes or carrots because these vegetables like the soil to be a little sticky. However, this light soil is perfect for growing garlic. Add a little more dirt from the yard to your raised bed.

4 If you are able to make a sausage shape without it breaking, your soil is excellent for gardening. You are going to have a great time!

How to know if the soil is chalky

Have you ever used chalk to write on a blackboard? It's made of limestone and can be found in certain soils. In chalky soils, gardening is not easy.

Here's one way to find out if your soil has a lot of limestone in it: carefully pour a little vinegar onto the ground. If the soil has limestone in it, you will see small foamy bubbles start to form. To reduce the amount of limestone in the soil, you will have to mix compost into it every year. Just like you did in your box garden!

Build seed bombs!

Take some clay or dirt from your yard and mix it with an equal amount of potting soil. Then add a mixture of flower seeds. You can make seed bombs as big as ping-pong balls and then, in the spring, throw them into the bushes around your yard. They'll grow all by themselves!

PLANTING CARROT SEEDS

You can plant carrot seeds "on the fly," which means that you can scatter them on top of the soil without making furrows. First, rake the ground to remove any stones or clods larger than marbles and to create a flat surface with thin soil.

1. Pour a few seeds from the packet (around 10) into a small hand seeder made of green transparent plastic.

Don't sow all of the seeds in the packet. You will have too many carrots in your raised bed and they won't have enough room to grow properly.

2. Crouch down, holding the seeder around 2 inches from the ground. Gently shake it to make the seeds slide out.

3 Cover the seeds with loose dirt, sprinkling it over them with your hands. A thin layer of dirt is plenty—just enough to hide the seeds.

4 Gently press down with the palm of your hand to make sure the seeds are buried.

Not *too* buried, otherwise they will suffocate and won't grow!

5 Finally, use a watering can with a fine spray head to water your seeds.

Thanks to its little holes, the fine spray head allows the water to come out like a light rain.

What happens next?

Water a little bit every day. The seedlings will come out of the ground around two weeks after you sow the seeds. About three months later, you can pull up the carrots and eat them!

PLANTING GREEN BEAN SEEDS

The bean plant takes up more room than a carrot, so you won't be able to put very many in a small box garden. If you really like beans, you can plant some in two small raised beds, either next to each other or separate. Green bean seeds are big enough to pick up one by one with your fingers. You will plant them in seed holes.

Water just enough to keep the soil cool and to keep it from hardening. If you don't, the roots will not be able to dig through the soil.

1. Dig two or three holes as big as the palm of your hand. Make them as deep as the second knuckle on your index finger.

2. Place three seeds in each hole and lay them flat, leaving around 1 inch between each seed.

3 Cover with dirt and press down gently with the palm of your hand or even with your foot.

4 Water with a watering can equipped with a fine spray head.

What happens next?

Water a little bit every day. The seedlings will quickly emerge from the ground, about a week after you plant the seeds. You can pick the first bean pods in around two months.

All kinds of seeds

All plants produce seeds. Some, like the seeds of the pansy, which is a plant that blooms in the spring, are very small. Others, like green bean seeds lined up in their pod, are on the larger side.

SEED RIBBONS AND MATS

Sometimes at the store next to the seed packets, you might find seeds sold in ribbons or rolls of thin paper.

1. In one of your raised beds, trace three furrows ½ inch deep with a hoe or a piece of wood. Leave a space as wide as your hand between each furrow.

2. Tear the ribbon with your hands into strips the same length as your furrows.

3. Lay the strips of ribbon at the bottom of each furrow and cover them with loose soil. Press down a little with your fingers, but not too hard.

A furrow? This is a long straight line dug in the ground.

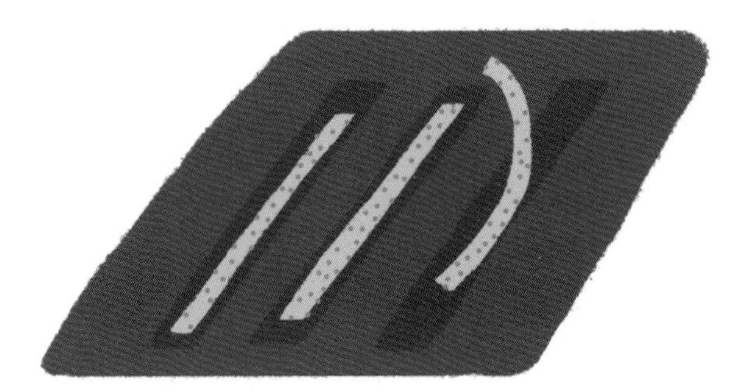

4 Water using a watering can equipped with a fine spray head. Do not soak the soil. You just need to keep it damp and prevent it from drying out.

So convenient!

Seed ribbons are practical because the paper around the seeds protects them from diseases and ensures that each seed has enough room to grow.

Isn't it incredible?

The largest seed in the world is the palm tree seed, which can weigh up to 45 pounds! It has a very funny shape—it looks a little like a butt!

The smallest seed comes from an orchid called Bletilla. In our vegetable gardens, the smallest seeds belong to the celery plant: in a single gram you can find 2,500 seeds!

PLANTING FLOWERS AND VEGETABLES WITH ROOT BALLS

If you want to have flowers and vegetables more quickly instead of waiting for seeds to grow, you can plant them as baby plants that already have root balls. These baby plants come from seeds that sprouted in small pots filled with soil.

Water the dirt well before and after you place the baby plant in the ground.

PLANTING SWISS CHARD

Where? Preferably in the sun

When? May and June

Watering? Regularly

1 Without removing the pot, always begin by submerging the plant's root ball in a bowl or watering can filled with water.

Hold the root ball underwater as long as there are bubbles appearing on the surface of the water.

2 Now remove the pot gently to avoid breaking the root ball.

3 Use a trowel to dig a hole slightly larger than the root ball, then gently place the plant inside. The hole should not be deeper than the height of the root ball.

4 Press down the soil around the root ball.

5 Water a little around the root ball using a watering can with the fine spray head removed.

Isn't it incredible?

The bald cypress is a coniferous tree that grows in humid soil that is prone to flooding. To make sure its roots can still breathe, this tree develops roots above ground called pneumatophores that look like the stalagmites you find in caves.

The mangrove is a tree that grows in water. It has large roots shaped like stilts to help it breathe.

Some trees push their roots up to 165 feet (50 meters) into the ground!

Why can't I find baby radish or carrot plants?

Root vegetables that are grown for their large, edible roots don't like to grow in potting soil. They also don't like being disturbed once their seeds have been planted and would not appreciate being transferred to your box garden.

You also won't find bean or pea plants with root balls because these vegetables are easy to grow from seeds.

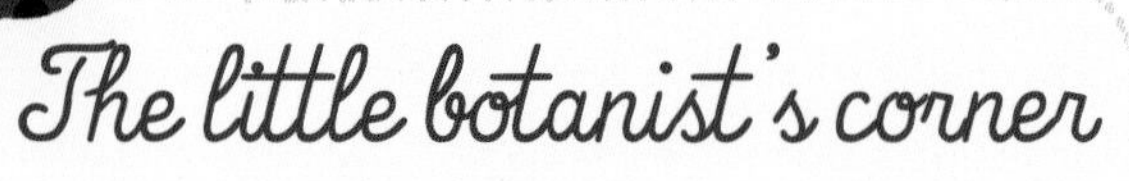

Roots are very important plant organs. They allow the plant to stand up straight by holding tightly onto the soil. They also work as pumps to draw in water that is filled with nutrients.

Now you understand why you should try not to break the root ball on baby plants—we don't want to damage their young roots just before they are planted. You should also now understand why watering is so important.

When you water, don't just wet the surface of the soil. Empty your whole watering can around each plant so the water can reach all the way to the roots.

ROOTS IN A GLASS

1 Fill a clear glass with a piece of absorbent cotton.

2 Wet the cotton just a little by pouring 2 tablespoons of water over it.

3 Place two bean seeds flat on top of the moistened cotton.

Place the glass somewhere in your house where it will get light but far away from radiators and direct sunlight.

4 Four or five days later, you will see roots emerge from each seed and you will be able to observe their pointed ends through the glass!

GARDENING WITH THE MOON

The moon is responsible for the phenomenon of the tides, which bring the ocean up onto the beach before pulling it back, a little or a lot, depending on the day. It also seems to influence plant growth. This is not easy to prove, but many gardeners have observed it.

There are two ways to observe the moon: first take a look at its shape, then notice how high it is in the sky.

SHAPE

1. Look at the moon one night before going to sleep. It may have a crescent shape, for example.

2. Two nights later, look at the moon again. Its crescent will be a little bigger.

3. Wait two more days and look again. The moon may look like an almost perfect circle. This is the full moon!

This period when the moon grows bigger and bigger is called waxing. When it is growing smaller and smaller each day, we say it is waning. This change in shape has very little impact on plants.

HEIGHT

1. Look at the moon one night before going to bed. Make a note of its position in the sky. You can do this by looking at how close the moon is to something outside that stays in one place, like a tree, telephone pole, or church steeple.

2. Wait two more days and look at the moon again, this time two hours later than the last time. The moon is no longer in the same place. It is either higher or lower in the sky. If it is higher, we say the moon is ascending, and if it is lower, it is descending.

It rises, then it falls, and so on . . .

When it is ascending, the moon helps seeds sprout, so this is a good time to plant seeds. In the descending phase, the moon helps roots do their work. This period is good for planting and repotting baby plants.

TAKING CUTTINGS

TAKING GERANIUM CUTTINGS

Planting a seed is usually all you need to grow a new plant, but you can also grow some plants from a tiny piece of the stem. This is called a cutting.

1 Ask an adult to cut pieces of geranium stem that are 4 inches long. These cuttings should be taken from the tips of the green shoots that have grown since the springtime.

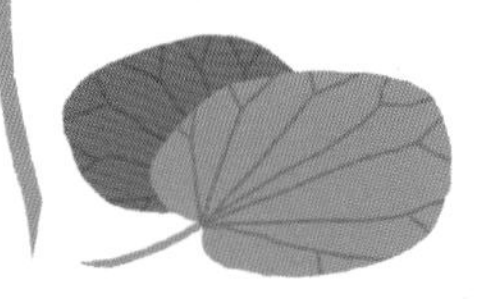

2 Remove all leaves from the cutting except for the two on top.

3 Plant your cuttings in rows in your box garden. Make sure they are about three finger-widths apart. Then water them a little bit.

Plant your cuttings deep enough that the soil almost reaches the two leaves on top.

The best time

Geranium cuttings are most likely to succeed if you plant them in August and September!

4 Ask an adult to cut the bottoms off of some plastic water bottles and place the top part of one bottle over each cutting. The bottles should still have their caps.

Plants that are easy to grow from cuttings

If you take their cuttings between August and September, carnations and even certain rosebushes will quickly take root. You can also take cuttings from dahlias, using the first stems that appear after the spring planting. Hydrangea, elderberry, and honeysuckle also grow well from cuttings. For these plants, take cuttings that are 10 inches long and bury three-quarters of each stem in loose soil. If you are not familiar with these plants, ask your grown-up if there are any in your yard.

Give it time to grow

If the cutting hasn't died after several weeks, this is a good sign. A successful cutting will produce new leaves or stems. But you have to be patient!

What happens next?

Never pull on a cutting to see if the roots have grown. You might break the roots and the cutting will not survive.

A FUNNY KIND OF CUTTING

If your grown-up buys a pineapple one day for dessert, ask them to keep the leaves so you can try growing a rather remarkable cutting.

1. Make sure that when your grown-up cuts the pineapple, they leave about ½ inch of fruit under the leaves.

2. Let the cutting sit on your kitchen counter overnight. Too much humidity will make it rot.

3. Find a pot a little wider than the pineapple and fill it with soil. Now place your cutting flat on top of the soil.

Your pineapple will turn into a pretty plant, but it won't produce any fruit!

4 Water well around your cutting.

5 Cover the cutting with a clear plastic bag and hold it in place by stretching a rubber band around the pot.

What happens next?

Keep your cutting in a pot indoors for at least three months without touching or watering it. This will keep it from rotting.

It worked!

After three months, a few of the outer leaves may have dried out, but you will see new leaves appear at the center of the plant. If this is not the case, new plants might be developing around the cutting. Either way, your cutting has succeeded, and you now have a pineapple plant. Bravo!

WATERING WITHOUT WASTING

At certain times of year, it doesn't rain enough for garden plants. You will have to make sure you water the plants in your raised bed yourself. It is important to learn how to do this without wasting water.

TIPS FOR WATERING MY RAISED BED

You may not have time to water every day, or you may forget. To be sure that your plants don't die of thirst, here are a few simple things you can do:

The upside-down bottle

Collect empty plastic water bottles that still have their caps.

1. Using a small hammer and nail, make a hole in each cap and screw them back onto the bottles.

2 Ask an adult to cut off the bottom of each bottle.

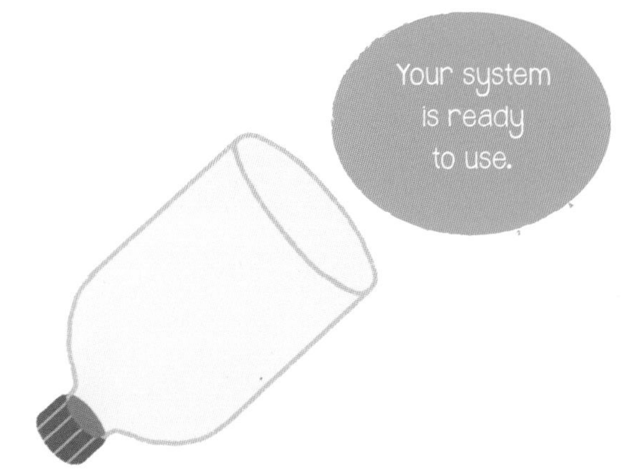

3 Push the bottles into the soil of your box garden with the cap facing down until the neck of the bottle is covered.

4 Use your watering can to gently pour water into each bottle until the bottle is about three-quarters full.

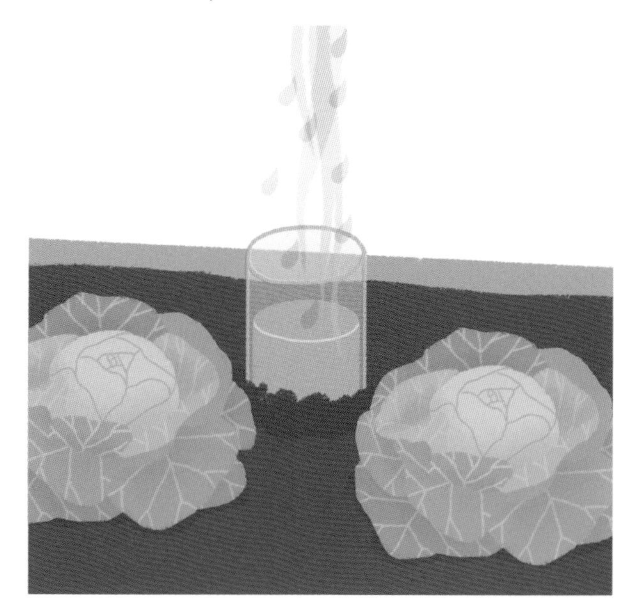

What happens next?

The water will slowly drip into the soil through the hole you made in the cap. This trick will last several days!

The buried pot

Find a few ceramic pots that are 4 to 6 inches wide.

1 Make sure that each pot has a hole in the bottom. Place a flat stone in the bottom of the pot on top of the hole.

2 Bury each pot in your box garden until just the upper lip is showing.

3 Fill the pots with water from a watering can.

Plan on using one bottle or pot for two plants. If you have two tomato plants, for example, place your bottle or pot in between them. This will provide both plants with enough water.

What happens next?

Water will slowly drip through the hole in the pot by sneaking under the stone you placed in the bottom.

Saving water from the bathroom

In the bathroom, you use water to wash your hands and brush your teeth. This "used" water leaves through the drain in the sink. But it's a shame to waste this water when it could be used to water your raised bed! Just because it has a little soap or toothpaste in it doesn't mean the plants won't drink it!

- When you use the sink, you can plug the drain and use the cut-off bottom of a plastic bottle to scoop out the water into a watering can when you have finished washing.
- You can also place a small bowl in the sink to collect the used water directly. This is easier because you only have to carry it to the yard to water your plants.

The right time to water

When it is very sunny, heat makes water evaporate just like it does in a pot on the stove, even though you may not be able to see it. Because of this, watering when it is very hot is a waste of water. In the summer, when you're watering by hand with your watering can, or filling your pots and bottles, do it in the evening just before going to eat dinner.

FEEDING MY PLANTS

WHAT KIND OF FOOD SHOULD I GIVE MY PLANTS?

In general, everything plants need to eat is in the soil. But in a yard, and especially in a small box garden, if you are growing a lot of plants, the food supplies may run out quickly. So, you will need to go shopping and bring back some fertilizer.

1. Water the entire surface of your raised bed the day before you plan to use the fertilizer.

2. Sprinkle the fertilizer over the entire garden as evenly as possible, carefully following the instructions on the container about how much to use.

3 Mix the fertilizer into the soil using a pitch fork. That's it!

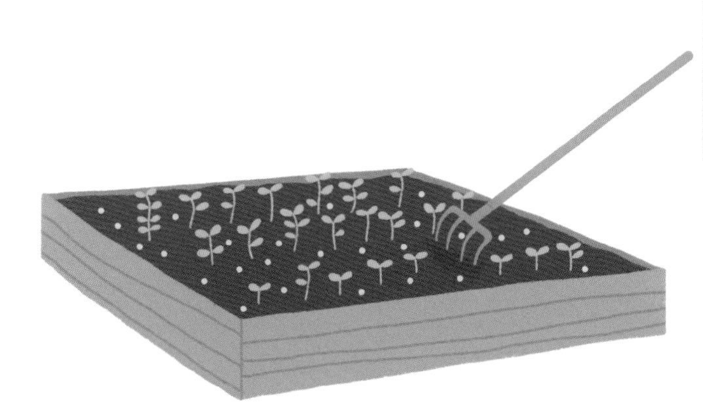

Not every day!

Remember, plants don't need to be fed every day or every two or three days like a goldfish. Fertilizer should only be used once a year!

Playing with marbles

There are so many different packs and bags of fertilizer at the store! Ask your grown-up to find a complete fertilizer labeled "slow release." It comes in the form of small yellow balls that are easy to see on top of the dirt, which will keep you from sprinkling too many of them. These balls melt very slowly into the soil to bring the roots their food a little at a time, whenever they need it.

They feed themselves with their roots

The roots of the plant draw water up from the soil. This water contains many tiny things that we aren't able to see, but the plant absolutely has to have them in order to grow.

MUSSELS AND OYSTERS ON THE MENU

If your grown-ups happen to be preparing oysters or mussels, ask them if you can keep the empty shells. Just make sure the shells have cooled down from cooking!

These shells come from the ocean, so they contain enormous amounts of mineral salts like calcium, sodium, and boron, which plants need in small quantities. This is why they make great fertilizer.

1. Wash the shells well to remove any bits of shellfish, sauce, lemon, or garlic.

2. Spread out the shells on the ground.

3. Break them into tiny pieces with a hammer or rock.

4 When you have broken the shells into very small pieces, sprinkle them on top of the soil in your garden.

5 Mix the shell pieces into the soil with a pitch fork.

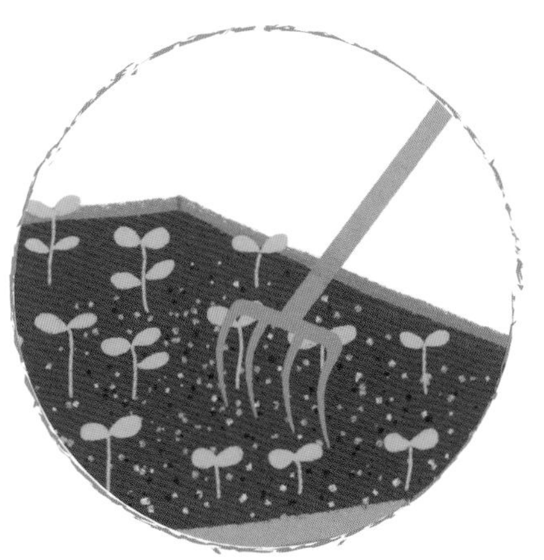

The little botanist's corner

Plants always eat a varied meal. This meal is usually made up of three things: nitrogen (to make plants grow and keep them green), potassium, and phosphorus (which help form roots, flowers, and fruit). The meal may contain many other elements that the plant uses in smaller amounts depending on what it needs at the time. These elements are calcium, magnesium, iron, etc.

In the same way that human blood can be analyzed with a blood test, soil can be analyzed to find out exactly what it contains.

MAKING MY COMPOST

A compost pile is a mound of plant and mineral waste that worms and other small creatures feed on, break down, and slowly decompose to transform it into a kind of soil.

The best way to make your own compost pile is to build another raised bed like the one you already have for growing vegetables. Just use the boards to assemble a square bed, and this time don't add any dirt.

1. Start by thoroughly watering the ground inside your compost bed.

2. Whenever you have plant waste, throw it on your compost pile.

Fruit and vegetable peelings, walnut and hazelnut shells, dead leaves, some grass clippings, and little pieces of broken twigs will form the base of your compost.

3 Stir your compost pile once a month, watering as you go to make sure the pile is always a little damp.

4 When your raised bed is full, stop adding plant waste but continue stirring and making sure it stays damp.

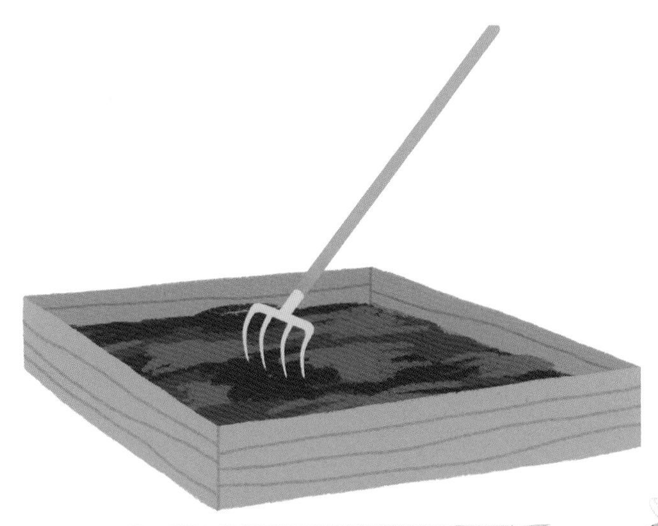

This is not a garbage dump!

Do not put leftover food, pieces of meat, or domestic animal litter in your compost pile. This will give your compost a bad odor and could attract rats and other animals.

It smells like the forest!

When the compost is ready to be used, you will no longer be able to see the pieces of wood, leaves, or peelings you had in the beginning. Instead, the pile will be totally black, a little damp, and will have the same smell you find in the forest.

What happens next?

After a few months, you can mix your compost into the soil in your box garden. Your soil will become more fertile and your vegetables will grow better.

WHO ARE THESE VISITORS?

In any garden, and even in a small box garden, in addition to the plants you have sown or planted, there are lots of things that show up all by themselves: weeds, small creatures, and even your dog or cat!

Weeds are growing between my plants

If you have a lot of weeds, you can pull them out by hand. Just use gloves if they are prickly ones like nettles.

Bugs are eating everything!

Aphids

Aphids are small creatures that can damage your plants. They are tiny but still easy to see, and they usually stick together on the tips of plant stems. To get rid of them, just break off the piece of stem where they have collected and crush them with your foot.

The leaves have not been eaten because aphi only suck on them.

Caterpillars

One creature you should worry about in any garden, especially a small one, is the caterpillar, or butterfly larva. Caterpillars spend their time devouring the leaves of many garden plants.

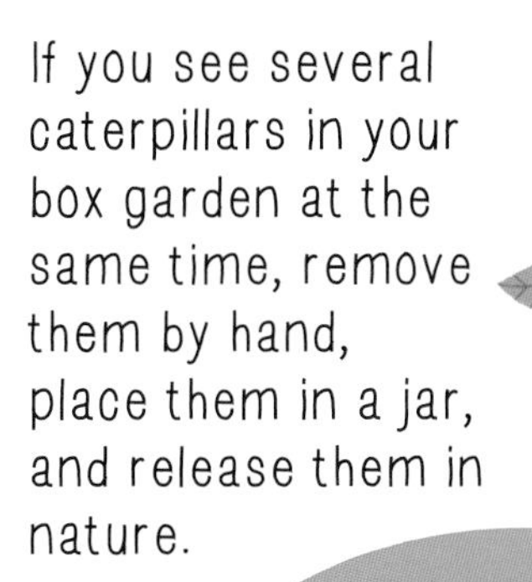

If you see several caterpillars in your box garden at the same time, remove them by hand, place them in a jar, and release them in nature.

Ladybugs are more than just cute little creatures. They are also great friends of gardeners because their larvae eat a lot of aphids!

Slugs

Slugs are a gardener's number-one enemy! There are very small ones that you can hardly see, and others as big as your thumb, but you will rarely notice them because they attack at night while you're sleeping. They snack on many different plants and can destroy them in a single night.

If you find traces of slime in your box garden one day, place an old plate on top of the soil and fill it with beer. Slugs love this drink and will eventually drown in it.

I'm a baby ladybug.

BUILDING A SCARECROW

A scarecrow is a kind of puppet that doesn't move and looks like a full-sized human. You can make one out of just about anything. If you stick one in the middle of your garden, it should frighten any birds and keep them from coming to peck at whatever seeds you just planted.

1. Find two pieces of wood. One of them should be about three times longer than the other.

2. Form a cross with the two pieces of wood and tie them together with string using a square knot (as shown on page 12).

3. Place your cross in the corner of your raised bed so it doesn't get in the way when you're taking care of your plants.

4. Ask your grown-up to give you an old shirt or sweatshirt you don't wear anymore. If possible, it should be a bright color, like red.

5. Dress your cross with the old clothes.

6. An old deflated ball will make an excellent head for the top of the cross. Finish off your scarecrow with a straw hat or baseball cap.

To make it more effective, change your scarecrow's position about every three days.

DISCOVERING PERMACULTURE

This gardening style tries to mirror what happens in nature as much as possible. In the forest, for example, plants and animals live together and depend on each other: there are tall trees, then smaller ones, then bushes, then grass, then moss, etc., and at every level, there are animals who use these plants for shelter and food. This whole little world lives in harmony without humans ever getting involved.

LET NATURE DO ITS WORK

Permaculture is a way to try and make a garden self-sufficient. Dead leaves fall from the trees and keep the ground cool, earthworms make sure the soil is loose for the roots, the leaves decompose and transform into fertilizer for the plants, and the helpful creatures taking shelter in these leaves eat up the slugs, aphids, and other bugs before there are too many. . . . You, young gardener, are simply introducing fruit and vegetable plants into this cycle so they can benefit from this natural system.

LOTS OF DIFFERENT PLANTS

Have you heard of thujas? A lot of people plant and trim these evergreen trees to form green walls that keep neighbors from seeing inside their yards. Instead of planting these hedges, which don't really have a purpose, it's better to plant rows of trees and different kinds of bushes: some with flowers, others with fruit, some with thorns, some that are evergreen, and others that lose their leaves in winter. These kinds of hedges, made up of a mixture of plants, will attract plenty of animals–the architects of biodiversity.

Homes for insects, birds, hedgehogs, and snakes

Every creature has its own job in the garden: some carry pollen from the flowers you plant, while others eat weeds and unwanted bugs to make sure they don't snack on your plants. To help keep them in your garden, think about creating places for them to stay: hotels for insects, nests for birds, woodpiles for snakes, and piles of dead leaves for hedgehogs. Always put these shelters somewhere fairly private. That way, the animals will feel protected from their predators all year long!

TRIVIA

Does it matter how you lay a seed when planting it?

No. No matter how you lay the seed, the tiny root will emerge from the seed and grow down, and the little stem will grow up to come out of the soil.

WHAT DO THE LETTERS N, P, AND K ON FERTILIZER PACKETS STAND FOR?

- An abbreviation for Never Plant Kukumbers. ;)
- They stand for nitrogen (N), phosphorous (P), and potassium (K), the three major elements in plant food.

They stand for nitrogen, phosphorous, and potassium...

What flower should you plant right next to tomatoes?

Marigolds. The little worms that often eat the roots of the tomato plant do not like the marigold's strong odor. With these flowers nearby, your tomatoes will be left alone!

Is the tomato...?

- A fruit.
- A vegetable.

Both! The tomato is classified as a vegetable, but botanically speaking, the red part of the tomato plant that we eat is, in fact, its fruit.

What makes the ladybug so helpful in the garden?

Ladybug larvae are big aphid-eaters. The more ladybugs there are in a garden, the less necessary it is to use plant treatment products.

Which plant contains the scratchy hairs that pranksters use to tickle their friends' backs?

- The thistle.
- The dog rose.

The dog rose, or wild rose. Inside its red fruits, called rosehips, you will find the famous hairs that make people itch.

What kind of flower is an "iceberg"?

- A rose.
- An edelweiss.
- A snowdrop.

- *The snowdrop is a plant that grows from bulbs with white, bell-shaped flowers that bloom in early spring.*
- *The edelweiss is a hardy mountain plant with white and woolly flowers.*
- *The iceberg is a type of rose—one that has white flowers, obviously.*

What kind of fruit peel can be used as fertilizer?

Banana peel. It contains a lot of potassium, an element that is very useful for plants when their flowers bloom.

WHAT IS A REPEAT-FLOWERING PLANT?

- A plant that climbs walls all by itself.
- A plant that blooms or produces fruit at two different times of year.

A plant that blooms or produces fruit at two different times of year—once in June and again from August to September.

What are we doing when we pre-soak a plant?

- Watering it with a fine spray.
- Submerging the root ball in a bowl before planting it.

Pre-soaking a plant means submerging the root ball in a bowl before planting it.

MY VEGETABLES AND FRUITS

Don't plant vegetables in your box garden that take up too much room or are too hard to take care of. To help you choose which ones to plant, here's a little list of easy vegetables with advice on growing each one.

Chives

This plant produces a tuft of green shoots that we cut into tiny pieces to add flavor to omelettes and sour cream. It is also a very pretty plant with pink and purple flowers that look like pompoms.
Buy in pot.
One plant is enough.

Planting: In March or April.
Harvesting: One month after planting. Just break off a few leaves with your fingers. Four or five is enough to flavor a dish!

To keep the roots from tasting too spicy, make sure the dirt is never dry in the time between sowing and harvesting!

Radishes

All children know and love radishes! The great thing about this vegetable is that it takes up very little room and it can grow between lettuce or carrot plants. Don't plant all the seeds in the packet at once. Instead, plant them a little at a time, around twenty seeds every two weeks.
Buy in seed packets.
One packet is enough.

Sowing: From March to June.
Harvesting: One to two months after sowing. Pull on the leaves to remove the roots from the soil one by one.

Lettuce

This is the classic salad ingredient. There are green-leaved varieties, of course, but there are others that have purple leaves, smooth leaves, or wavy leaves. You can sow lettuce seeds, but it is easier to plant baby lettuce plants with root balls.
Buy as plants. (Lettuce is often sold with several small plants in one container called a flat. Ask your grown-ups if they'd like to share a flat with you.)
Three plants is enough for your raised bed.

Planting: From April to June.
Harvesting: One and a half months after planting.

Ready to cut

Lettuce is usually harvested by cutting the plant with a knife just above the ground, under the leaves. It's a good idea to let an adult take care of this step. There is, however, another kind of lettuce called leaf lettuce with leaves you can pick one at a time by hand. After you pick the leaves, new ones appear and you can harvest again.

In each row, always harvest the largest carrots first. This will leave room for the others to grow bigger, too.

Carrots

With its famous orange root, the carrot is the queen of summer vegetables and needs no introduction. Don't sow all the seeds in the packet at once, though—plant them little by little over the course of two weeks.
Buy in seed packets.
One packet is enough.

Sowing: From April to July.
Harvesting: Three months after sowing. To make it easier to remove each root, push a small spade into the ground just next to the carrot, then wiggle it out while you use your other hand to pull on the leaves.

Swiss chard

With its wide green leaves and red veins, this plant is as beautiful to look at as it is good to eat! There are even some varieties with orange veins.
Buy in pot.
One is enough.

Planting: In May or June.
Harvesting: One and a half months after planting. Harvest by snipping off the most developed leaves with a pair of pruning shears. It is best to let your parents do this.

Cherry tomatoes

This is the vegetable king of your raised bed! Save it a nice spot at the bottom of the trellis so you can attach its branches to it over time. You can sow seeds, but it is quicker and easier if you buy the plants already in pots.
Buy in pots.
One or two plants is enough.

Planting: In May.
Harvesting: The first tomatoes can be harvested two months after planting.

Pick the tomatoes as they ripen. Pull down gently to remove them from their stems.

Strawberries

What's a garden bed without a few strawberries to munch on? Plant a few strawberry plants along the edge of your raised bed so you can pick them easily without your other vegetables getting in the way.
Buy as plants.
Five plants is enough. Be sure to choose repeat-flowering varieties.

Planting: In September.
Harvesting: From June to September. Pick the berries a few at a time as soon as they are totally red. Pinch their stems between the nails of your thumb and index finger.

Repeat-flowering: yes or no?

A repeat-flowering variety produces fruit once in May and June, then again from mid-August until September. Varieties that are not repeat flowering only produce fruit in May. Two good repeat-flowering varieties are the garden strawberry (Mara des Bois) and the woodland strawberry.

Green beans

Green beans are not always green! They also come in yellow and even purple! They are easy to grow and don't require much work until it is time to harvest.
Buy in seed packets.
One packet is enough.

Sowing: From May to July.
Harvesting: Two months after sowing, from July to September. Gently pull on the beans with one hand while holding the stem with the other hand to avoid pulling everything out at once.

MY FLOWERS

Here is a selection of easy-to-grow flowers that you can mix in with your vegetables or plant in a separate box garden.

RULES TO FOLLOW WHEN PICKING FLOWERS

Follow these rules and you'll be able to enjoy your bouquet long after you put it in a vase!

First rule: Always cut flowers in the morning, before the sun hits them. They will be full of sap and in fine form!

Second rule: Try to pick flowers that are in the bud stage and just starting to open. They will last much longer in a vase. You can always add two or three opened flowers to give your bouquet some immediate pop.

Third rule: Cut flowers with pruning shears or a pair of scissors and cut on a diagonal to increase the surface area. This will help the flowers absorb more water. It's best to let an adult take care of this step.

Fourth rule: Place the cut flowers in a vase with water as quickly as possible to keep the cut from drying out and getting clogged. Remember to pull off any low leaves along the stem that might end up underwater. There should not be any leaves in the water—they will rot.

Fifth rule: Empty a flower preservative packet into the water. Add water to the vase as time passes and the water level lowers.

Ornamental onion

This plant looks like the garlic we use in the kitchen, but it is better known for the astonishing purple ball-shaped blooms set atop its tall stems.
Buy as bulbs.
At least seven for a stunning result.

Planting: In October or November.
Flowering: From May to July.

After blooming, the stem and flower dry out, but the bulb stays in the soil to produce flowers the following year.

Daffodils

Daffodils are not as famous as tulips, but they do bloom in the month of February! The bulbs stay in the ground and bloom again every year.
Buy as bulbs.
Buy in packs of fifteen—this will look spectacular!

Planting: In September.
Flowering: From February to April.

Cosmos

This graceful and typically pink flower is often seen filling whole fields along the road. Cosmos seeds have to be sown every year because the plant dies in the winter.
Buy in seed packets.
One packet is enough.

Sowing: In April.
Flowering: From June to September.

Dahlias

This plant grows from a large root called a tuber. Since dahlias are afraid of frost, they are usually pulled up after blooming to be replanted in the spring.
Buy in bags.
One plant is enough for a raised bed.

Planting: In April or May.
Flowering: From August to October.

Sunflowers

If you can only choose one large flower variety and decide to plant sunflowers, they are likely to become your garden box's main attraction— who knows, they might even turn into the stars of your whole backyard!
Buy in seed packets.
One packet is enough because you only need a few seeds.

Sowing: In April or May.
Flowering: From July to October.

California Poppy

This orange poppy has a shape that looks more like a tulip.
It blooms for a very long time.
Buy in seed packets.
One packet is enough.

Sowing: In April or May.
Flowering: From June to October.

Marigolds

This plant is the king of flowering because its blooms last from May to October. You can plant marigold seeds, but it's easy to find these as potted plants that will bloom quickly.
Buy as plants.
Three to five plants is enough.

Planting: In April.
Flowering: From May to October.

Nasturtiums

This is a wonderful plant that requires almost no maintenance. Just sow a few seeds here and there and you will eventually see lots of leaves followed by orange flowers that will last until autumn! The flowers make seeds that fall to the ground and produce new flowers the following year.
Buy in seed packets.
One packet is enough.

Sowing: In April or May.
Flowering: From May to October.

Geraniums

We call this plant a "geranium," but its real name is actually "pelargonium." It is most often used in pots and flower boxes. Some houses have geraniums on every windowsill and even on the garden gate! But you can also plant some in your raised bed.
Buy in pots.
One to three plants is enough for a nice look.

Planting: May.
Flowering: From June to October.

MY GARDENING CALENDAR

January	• Let your garden box rest under straw.	
February	• Let your garden box rest under straw.	
March	• Sow radish seeds.	• Plant chives.
April	• Sow carrot seeds. • Sow radish seeds. • Plant chives. • Plant lettuce. • Sow nasturtium seeds.	• Sow cosmos seeds. • Sow poppy seeds. • Sow sunflower seeds. • Plant dahlias. • Plant marigolds.
May	• Sow carrot seeds. • Sow green bean seeds. • Sow radish seeds. • Plant lettuce. • Plant Swiss chard.	• Plant cherry tomatoes. • Sow nasturtium seeds. • Sow poppy seeds. • Plant dahlias. • Plant geraniums.

June	• Sow carrot seeds. • Sow green bean seeds. • Sow radish seeds. • Plant lettuce. • Plant Swiss chard.
July	• Sow carrot seeds. • Sow green bean seeds.
August	• Build your raised beds.
September	• Plant strawberries. • Plant daffodils.
October	• Plant ornamental onion.
November	• Plant ornamental onion.
December	• Let your garden box rest under straw.

INDEX

Aphids, caterpillars, slugs, ladybugs - 44-45

Beans - 20, 55
Biodiversity - 49

California poppy - 58
Carrots - 18, 53
Chalky soil - 17
Cherry tomatoes - 54
Chives - 52
Climbing plants - 12
Clods - 14
Compost - 15, 42
Cosmos - 57
Cuttings - 30-33

Daffodil - 57
Dahlia - 58

Dibble - 8

Earthworms - 14

Fertilizer - 38
Furrow - 22

Geraniums - 30, 59

Hand seeder - 18
Handles - 9
Hoe - 7, 22

Lettuce - 53

Marigold - 59
Moon - 28
Mussels and oysters - 40

Nasturtium - 59

Ornamental onion - 57

Permaculture - 48
Pitch fork - 6, 15, 39, 41
Planting - 24

Radish - 52
Raised bed - 10
Rake - 6
Root balls - 24
Roots - 8, 26, 39

Scarecrow - 46
Seed bombs - 17
Seed holes - 20
Seed ribbons - 22
Shovel - 15
Soil - 14
Sowing seeds - 18, 20
Strawberries - 55
Sunflower - 58
Swiss chard - 24, 54

Thujas - 49
Tools - 6
Trowel - 7, 25

Watering can, watering - 8, 24, 34-37

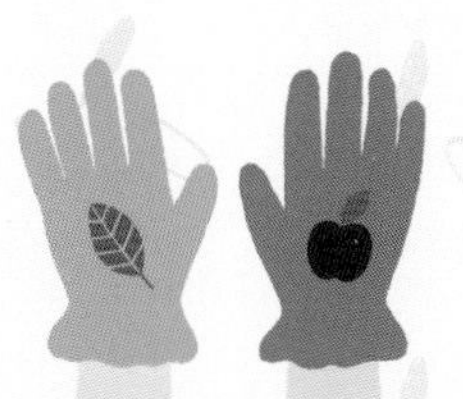